ISLAM AND THE GOSPEL

Comprising

ISLAM COMES TO BRITAIN
John Coonan

1979

OUR MUSLIM NEIGHBOURS
William Burridge

1987

CAN WE TRUST THE GOSPELS
– A LETTER TO MY MUSLIM BROTHERS

John Wijngaards

1985

CATHOLIC TRUTH SOCIETY
PUBLISHERS TO THE HOLY SEE

Christians and Muslims
have many things in common.
First, of course, faith in the same
God, the one God,
who created the world…

Mgr John Coonan was a priest of Westminster diocese;
William Burridge (1909-2000) was a priest of the White Fathers;
John (Hans) Wijngaards was formerly a priest
of the Mill Hill Missionaries.

CTS ONEFIFTIES

Originally published as *Islam comes to Britain*, 1979; *Our Muslim Neighbours*,
1987; *Can we trust the Gospels – a letter to my Muslim brothers*, 1985 (previously
Objections to the Gospels, 1981).

Published by The Incorporated Catholic Truth Society,
40-46 Harleyford Road, London SE11 5AY

www.ctsbooks.org
Copyright © 2017 The Incorporated Catholic Truth Society.

ISBN 978 1 78469 537 8

ISLAM COMES TO BRITAIN

John Coonan

ISLAM COMES TO BRITAIN

John L. Coonan, S.T.L.

Mosques in London — and Rome

Although there has been an Islamic presence in the United Kingdom for very many years and a mosque in Woking, in Surrey, the dramatic appearance in 1977 of the magnificent new mosque in Regent's Park, London, with its golden dome glittering through the surrounding trees, has awakened many Christians to the growing strength of Islam in this country. The proposal that a mosque of equal size and beauty be built in Rome is a further indication of Islam's European growth. To make, with due respect, a comparison: England now has more Muslims than Methodists.

In Europe, besides Turkey, which is officially European though partly in Asia and has 35 million inhabitants, there are six million native Muslims spread over Yugoslavia, Albania, Bulgaria, Greece, Cyprus and Romania. Besides this, there are between three and four million migrant Muslim workers in other Western European countries. Apart from Russia and Turkey, there are an estimated nine to ten million Muslims in Europe, a number of whom are converts to that faith. It is therefore clear that Islam is not a distant religion which is only the concern of missionaries and lecturers in comparative religion but of practical interest to all Christians. Our next-door neighbours might as easily be Muslims, born or converted, as anything else. To appreciate their point of view with the sympathy and understanding necessary for human contact, some knowledge of their faith and its background is essential.

Mohammed

Orphaned very young, Mohammed (570–632 A.D.) belonged to a poor tribe in Mecca, Arabia, the Banu Hashim, a subdivision of the wealthy Quraysh. He was the prophet through whom, according to Islam, God revealed its teachings. These teachings were dictated by God through the Angel Gabriel to Mohammed and 'recited' or written down in a book called the Koran (Qur'an), which means 'recital.' Followed by a few loyal adherents but rejected by the majority of polytheistic Meccans, who persecuted and boycotted them, Mohammed left Mecca for Medina, some 200 miles away, in 622. This is known as the year of the *Hegira* (Emigration), and, from it, Islam dates its years. Helped by a temporary pact with three Jewish groups, Mohammed established an Islamic state at Medina, and returned to conquer Mecca and become the rallying point of the Arab tribes of the Arabian peninsula. He died at the age of 63, having finally united all the tribes of Arabia under one emblem, the Crescent, and one religion, Islam.

A number of religious, political and economic factors, combined with the genius of the Caliphs, the successors of Mohammed, led to the successful conquest for Islam, in considerably less than a century, of Palestine, Syria, Mesopotamia, Egypt, North Africa and the south of Spain. They crossed the Pyrenees but were defeated by Charles Martel at Tours, in 732, a hundred years after the death of

Mohammed, a defeat which arrested their Western conquests. In the eighth and ninth centuries, they conquered Afghanistan and a large part of India; and, in the twelfth century, they had already become the absolute masters of Western Asia, North Africa and Sicily, though they were beginning to lose their hold on Spain. Though the Arab Muslims were conquered by the Mongols and Turks in the thirteenth century, both these groups accepted the religion of Islam, and, in the fifteenth century, overthrew the Christian Byzantine Empire (1453). From the stronghold in Constantinople, the capital of that Empire, they threatened the German Empire, but were defeated by John Sobieski at the very gates of Vienna and driven back across the Danube, in 1683. Apart from Turkey and Albania, no European country is Muslim, but in Africa and Asia there are a number of Muslim countries, and many more have small to very large Muslim minorities. A few, though not official Muslim states, have Muslim majorities. The estimated world population of Muslims is disputed, with an upper limit of one thousand million quoted by the Saudis but the generally accepted estimate is half this. Much depends on how one reckons the numbers in China and the Soviet Union.

The Teaching

The two main sources of Muslim teaching are the *Qur'an* and Tradition *(Sunna)*.

The Qur'an

The Qur'an is central to Islam. It was 'received' by Mohammed from God and 'recited' by him to his followers. It is a sacred book which is 'the very word of God', lasting from all eternity and unalterable. Nothing that is true can contradict it. Most Muslim children learn at least a few verses of it by heart.

Composed of 114 *surahs* or chapters, and preserved at first by simple memorising by Mohammed's first followers, it was quickly codified into a single definitive text which, nevertheless, admits of seven orthodox styles of recitation, which they do not regard as variants of the text. The *Qur'an* is regarded as a 'revealed' text, not an 'inspired' one.

That is, God did not speak through the words or use the literary style of another to convey his meaning. The words of the *Qur'an* are God's own words. So, methods of interpretation used, for instance, by modern biblical scholars, such as taking into consideration literary forms and the cultural context of the Bible, are not acceptable to Muslims in relation to the *Qur'an*. The author is God, not Mohammed. Dictated in Arabic, it cannot be translated officially into another language, though of course various unofficial translations do exist. Non-Arab Muslims are invited to learn Arabic, since the Muslim official prayers are always in that language. Unchangeable in its text, language and content, the *Qur'an* is for the Muslims at once Bible, Constitution, Civil Law, Penal Law, Code of Etiquette and Book of Liturgical Rubrics, summing up all the rules of Muslim good conduct. The very short opening chapter, which has been called the *Our Father* of Islam, since it appears so frequently in their devotions, reads thus:

"In the name of the Merciful, the Compassionate God. Praise be to God, the Lord of all creatures; the Most Merciful, the King of the Day of Judgment. Thee do we worship and of Thee do we beg assistance. Direct us in the right way, in the way of those to whom Thou has been gracious; not of those against whom Thou art incensed, nor of those who go astray."

Tradition (Sunna)

Constantly read, learnt by heart, and meditated upon, the *Qur'an* is the first formative element of the Muslim mentality. Next comes Tradition, the *Sunna*. This is a collection of short anecdotes about the Prophet describing, on the authority of his contemporaries, what he said, did or did not do in various situations. These anecdotes are called *Hadith*, and reflect the behaviour of the first Muslims, as the Epistles might be thought to reflect that of the first Christians. The *Sunna* appears as the way in which the first Muslims put into practice the teaching of the *Qur'an*, especially as that teaching was displayed in the life of the Prophet. The *Sunna*, 'evidence of tradition', joined itself to the 'evidence of scripture', and has become, down the centuries, an integral and much quoted part of Islamic culture.

Muslim Law (Shar'iah)

In its origins, Islam knows no distinction between religion and the state. It is one community. Its law deriving from the *Qur'an* covers therefore both religion and social life, as did the law of God in the Old Testament. Severe penalties are laid down in the *Qur'an:* e.g. the cutting-off of hands for stealing. In his lifetime, Mohammed was legislator, judge and executive, but when he died there was no further revelation. As the Muslim community grew to the proportions of an Empire and legal problems multiplied, a way had to be found to deal with them without violating the *Qur'an*.

As we have already seen, *Sunna*, or Tradition, was one source of such adaptation. Another was, and is, *Ijma*, agreement, defined as 'the public opinion of the Muslim community as expressed through its most learned jurists.' The justification for using *Ijma* is found in the statement in the *Qur'an* that, 'It is the duty of the Muslims to run their affairs on the basis of consensus.' Through this door, radical changes can be introduced. For example, circumcision, not mentioned in the *Qur'an,* became, through *Ijma,* a universal Muslim practice.

A third source of Islamic Law is *Qiyas,* or analogy. By it, a comparison is made between a matter dealt with in the *Qur'an* or by the Prophet and one which arises at the present time. A logical conclusion is then drawn and becomes binding. One example is the extension of the prohibition of wine in the *Qur'an* to include all alcoholic drinks. Wherever a Muslim community exists in any strength, it feels that its life should be governed by Islamic Law *(Shar'iah)* which, through the ways mentioned above, can be adjusted to modern needs and situations.

The Credo of Islam

The basic belief of Islam, 'There is no god but God, and Mohammed is his prophet', includes, for Muslims, the following beliefs and practices.

God

There is one God who is absolutely distinct from the world, and, although He is 'closer to us than our jugular vein,' He is in no sense within creation. He is totally transcendent and not immanent. We do not know the nature of God, only the law of God. Our attitude to that law should be total submission. The word Islam means just that: total submission.

'God does not beget and is not begotten.' The doctrine of the Blessed Trinity is rejected because it is seen as incompatible with the unity of God. The doctrine of the Incarnation, that God the Son became Man, is rejected as against both the unity of God and the absolute transcendence of God. God is contemplated and worshipped by Muslims through the mystery of His ninety-nine 'beautiful names' found in the *Qur'an* and Tradition *(Sunna)*.

'He is the most Merciful; He is the King, the Holy, the Giver of peace; the Faithful, the Guardian, the Powerful, the Strong, the Most High, the Creator, the Maker, the Former. He hath most excellent names; He is the Mighty, the Wise' *(Qur'an 59)*.

God rewards good and punishes evil deeds. He is merciful and easily propitiated by repentance.

Angels

The angels are the pure worshippers of God. They are also the messengers to men transmitting His revelation to them as did Gabriel to Mohammed. Their function is also to record the acts of men and examine them at the hour of death. One of them fell, because he refused to obey God's order to the angels to prostrate themselves before Adam *(Qur'an 7-12)*. Since then, with his demons, Satan tempts men by every means away from God to destruction. There are also intermediary spirits between angels and devils, to whom, it would seem, Mohammed was also sent.

Sacred Books

Muslims believe that there are four known 'Sacred Books,' through which God has made His message known: the *Torah* (the first five books of the Old Testament), the Psalms, the Gospel (singular), and the *Qur'an*.

The *Qur'an* abrogates and renders useless the previous books. In any case, the previous books, as they exist now, do not teach the true doctrine of the originals but are corruptions of them.

Prophets

In His mercy, God sends prophets to mankind at intervals. A distinction is made between 'great prophets' and 'minor prophets'. The former are the Messengers. They are: Abraham, 'the friend of God, the founder of religion that is in spirit and in truth'; Moses, the mouth-piece of God; Jesus, the Messiah, Son of Mary, Master of the Apostles and of Christians. Finally, Mohammed, 'the soul of the Prophets'; surely, he is the most perfect and the most just, sent to all men 'to perfect their religion' *(Qur'an* 5,3).

Many of the minor prophets are taken from the Old Testament, e.g. Adam, Noah, Jacob, David, etc. Others are from the Arab religious tradition; all proclaim the basic message of monotheism.

Resurrection and Last Judgment

All creatures, angels, *jinns,* mankind, and animals, will be resurrected. All men will have to submit to the last judgment. The punishment of the impenitent wicked will be fearful, the reward of the faithful great. The Day of Resurrection and Judgment will be preceded and accompanied by seventeen fearful signs, some identical with those mentioned in the New Testament. Both the punishment of the wicked and the happiness of the just are portrayed in very physical and material terms.

Predestination

The *Qur'an* states, 'God guides where He will and leads astray where He will' (74, 31); and, again, 'Let him who wills take, then, a road towards his Lord; but you will not will it except God wills it' (76, 29-30).

On the other hand, it also states, 'On that day every man will be repaid for what he has done' (53, 59); and again, 'the truth emanates from your Lord; whoever wills it let him be a believer and whoever wills it let him be an unbeliever' (18, 23).

This tension between predestination and free will, which is also known to Christians, has, in the past, for Muslims, been heavily weighted in favour of predestination. Contemporary Islam is tending to show more emphasis on liberty and free will.

Concerning Christ

An exceptional place is given to Christ Our Lord in the *Qur'an*, though, in view of the nature of the Islamic conception of God, His Divinity is denied. He is placed high in the ranks of the prophets, but He is only a man. He was born of Mary, with no human father, through the direct intervention of the creative word of God. He was sent as God's prophet to the sons of Israel; He brought the Gospel of pure monotheism, performed miracles, was rejected by the Jews, who tried to crucify Him, but He was rescued by God, who took Him to Himself until His return at the end of time, of which He will be the forerunner.

While the *Qur'an* expresses esteem for Christians and encourages friendly relations, even dialogue, it makes a positive attack on Christian doctrine concerning the Trinity and the Divinity of Christ, and claims that the Church has falsified

Christ's teaching. However, the versions of these doctrines attacked are not those of orthodox Christianity, since the only contact Mohammed had with Christians was with those who were heretical on these points.

Concerning Our Lady

One of the remarkable features of the *Qur'an* is what it has to say about Our Lady. Although it relies on apocryphal or legendary sources, it presents her with real feeling and reverence. She is, it says, the descendant of the prophetic lineage of Abraham and Jacob; her mother dedicated her to God before her birth; she grew up in the Temple under the guardianship of Zachary, and is provided miraculously with food. The angel appears to her and announces the virginal birth of a holy child, as in the Gospel account. She is spoken of as Virgin of Virgins, who conceived by the breath of God. With her Son, who is habitually referred to as the Son of Mary in the *Qur'an,* she is a sign to the world. In defence of her, a passage reads, 'We curse them for their unbelief and for uttering against Mary a great calumny.'

The Practising Muslim

Besides holding these beliefs, a practising Muslim will endeavour to fulfil a number of obligations laid down in the *Qur'an* and Tradition.

The Profession of Faith

Every Muslim must make the profession of Faith known as the *Shahada:* 'There is no god but God, and Mohammed is His

Prophet.' This declaration, to be effective, must be a genuine expression of belief and not merely external. When dying, a Muslim, turning his face towards Mecca if he can, reaffirms this belief as his final witness and as summing up the essentials of the Muslim faith.

Ritual Prayers

Five times each day, at dawn, midday, mid-afternoon, sunset, and later in the evening, the faithful Muslim prays, generally using a prayer-mat for this purpose and always turning towards Mecca. To perform the prayer properly the Muslim must be 'pure' in body, clothes, and with regard to the place of prayer. There are certain washings and ritual gestures by which this purity is attained. The prayer is composed of a number of postures, gestures and invocations expressed in liturgical units called *rak'a-s*. Each prayer will contain two, three or four of these, and a passage from the *Qur'an* is recited in each.

At midday on Friday, they should be performed, by men only, in the mosque. Women pray in public but separated from the men: thus the Central London mosque has a separate Ladies' Gallery, screened from the main body of the church.

Fasting

This is commended at all seasons but is of obligation only in the month of Ramadan, the ninth month of the Muslim liturgical year. In Ramadan, the fast begins at dawn and ends at sunset. During the night, food may be taken, and communal visiting and feasting is common.

Pilgrimage

Once in a lifetime, if he has the means and the strength to go, a Muslim should make the pilgrimage *(hajj)* to Mecca. While there, he wears the 'sacred dress', a single, unsewn length of cloth held round the waist by a knotted cord, and with one end draped over the shoulder. He honours the *Ka'ba,* or temple, by walking round it seven times in prayer. The Ka'ba, supposed to have been built by Abraham, is a pre-Islamic temple which Mohammed restored to the worship of the one God. Because of the vast number of pilgrims from many different countries, the pilgrimage reinforces the *umma,* or sense of world-wide Muslim community.

Almsgiving

Giving alms to the poor is highly commended by Muslim law, and is obligatory on the feast day after Ramadan. Originally, one-twelfth of the income of each believer was transferred to the 'community funds' for the poor and the needy. Modern Islamic states often incorporate these alms in the taxes levied.

These five practices are called the five pillars of Islam. Joined to them are many recommendations about food and drink (pork is not eaten, nor alcohol drunk), burials, visits to cemeteries, marriages (polygamy and divorce are allowed), family life and social relations.

The Community of Islam

One of the great strengths of Islam lies in the fact that it is not only a religion but a community; a culture, a civilisation – *umma.*

Though, in the course of centuries, subjected to many outside influences in different parts of the world, it has an inner unity, a special character of its own, difficult to define or appreciate but which is none the less real. This sense of community can transcend ethnic difference. There are in the world eighty million Arab Muslims, who are, in a sense, the leaders of the Muslim world; but there are also 150 million Muslim Pakistanis and Indians, one hundred million Muslim Indonesians and about sixty million Muslims in Black Africa. In America, since 1930, the Black Muslim movement has led many Black Americans to become Muslims.

In spite of their cultural differences, and even if Islamic states are often opposed to each other politically, there is a wider underlying sense of community which springs from a shared view of man, his destiny and his relationship to God.

Although under pressure in modern times, it would be a mistake to think that this sense of community and the self-confidence it imparts to individuals and the group will not survive.

Christian Mission and Islamic 'Calling', Da'wah

Both Christianity and Islam are of their nature missionary religions, and, up to the present day, their relationship has been largely one of confrontation. There are bitter memories on both sides. Muslims remember the Crusades in the past, and point, in the present, to what they feel is the unfair use of aid for material development as a means of spreading Christianity.

The Christians, on the other hand, remember the *Jihad*, or Holy Wars, of the past, and complain of the closed nature of

Islamic society today which, in many Islamic countries, prevents the Gospel from being preached in a positive way, and creates an atmosphere in which converts are socially penalised if not physically assaulted.

As far as Catholics are concerned, the Vatican Council, in its Document *Nostra Aetate* (CTS Do 360), has set a new tone.

'Upon the Muslims, too, the Church looks with esteem. They adore one God, living and enduring, merciful and all-powerful, Maker of heaven and earth and Speaker to men. They strive to submit wholeheartedly even to His inscrutable decrees, just as did Abraham, with whom the Islamic faith is pleased to associate itself. Though they do not acknowledge Jesus as God, they revere Him as a prophet. They also honour Mary, His virgin mother; at times they call on her, too, with devotion. In addition, they await the day of judgement when God will give each man his due after raising him up. Consequently, they prize the moral life, and give worship to God especially through prayer, almsgiving, and fasting.

'Although in the course of the centuries many quarrels and hostilities have arisen between Christians and Muslims, this most sacred Synod urges all to forget the past and to strive sincerely for mutual understanding. On behalf of all mankind, let them make common cause of safeguarding and fostering social justice, moral value, peace, and freedom' (No. 3).

At the centre of the Church, in Rome, the Secretariat for Non-Christians, through books and pamphlets and meetings, tries to disseminate knowledge and understanding of Islam and other non-Christian religions. In England, the Catholic Church has so far not done very much by way of approaching the Muslims.

In general, one can say that the ecumenical approach is

more common at the intellectual or theological level than in the field, and that Christians are more concerned to make such an approach than Islam.

In this country, the Islamic Council and the Islamic Foundation in Leicester publish well-produced pamphlets directed at the Christians, stressing the position of Christ in Islam and drawing attention to beliefs held in common by Islam and Christianity. They also state the Islamic case in terms suitable to a Christian audience. There is here, then, a positive, active and self-confident apostolate by Islam in relation to Christianity in this country.

In the so-called mission fields, the situation varies considerably. In some Muslim states, active proclamation of the Gospel is not permitted beyond, perhaps, a Christian 'presence.' In others, more latitude is allowed, but converts are rare, and the social climate inevitably makes life difficult for them. Where there are very large Christian minorities or where Muslims form a substantial minority, the situation is easier.

After centuries of confrontation, it is obviously not an easy matter to adjust relationships on a purely ecumenical basis within a few years. Nevertheless, in the modern world, with its closely-knit communications system, its financial interdependence, with its secularist tendencies and pressures, the ecumenical approach is the only sensible one to adopt.

Besides, as we have seen, positive points of contact with Christianity, Islam confronts the materialism of our time with the uncompromising assertion of the primacy of God and spiritual values.

Islam shares with Christianity belief in:

1. One God;
2. The Last Judgment and future life;
3. The Resurrection;
4. The value of prayer, fasting and almsdeeds;
5. The virginity of our Lady;
6. Angels;
7. The existence of evil – the devil.
8. It gives a special place to our Lord as a prophet.

Islam differs from Christianity:

1. It does not accept the doctrine of the Trinity.
2. It rejects the Divinity of Christ.
3. It rejects His death on the Cross.
4. It rejects the claims of the Catholic Church.

Both religions are expansionist: the Catholic Church through mission, Islam through *Da'wah*, or calling.

Both, up to the present, have confronted each other; now, there is a growing understanding of the need for an ecumenical approach.

Islam is still, on the whole, fundamentalist; it takes the Qur'an as literally God's word without modification. There is, however, a growing feeling of the necessity for *aggiornamento*, for taking the core of the message of Islam and expressing it in different frameworks, without altering what is essential to it.

BIBLIOGRAPHY

1. *The Concise Encyclopaedia of Living Faiths: Islam,* Hutchinson.
2. *Guidelines for a Dialogue between Muslims and Christians,* Ancora Edition, Rome, Secretariat for Non-Christians, Rome.
3. Gibb, H.A.R., *Islam,* OUP paper.
4. Guillaume, *Islam,* Penguin.
5. Mahmoud-Harris, Mariyam, *World Religions in Britain: 1. Islam,* BCC, 29pp. 15p.
6. El-Droubie, R. *Islam,* Ward Lock, 65p.
7. Cragg, *The Mind of the Koran,* Allen & Unwin.
8. Watt, W.M., *Muhammed: Prophet and Statesman,* OUP 1961.
9. Rodinson, M., *Muhammed,* Pelican.
10. Padwick, C., *Muslim Devotions.*
11. Cragg, K., *Alive to God.*
12. W.C.C., *Christian-Muslim Dialogue,* 1972.
13. W.C.C., *Christians Meeting Muslims,* 1977.
14. Brown, David, *A New Threshold,* BCC.
15. Parrinder, G., *Jesus in the Quran,* Faber, 1965.
16. El-Droubie, R., *A Muslim view of Jesus and Christianity,* Islamic Cultural Centre.
17. Schuon, Frithjof, *Understanding Islam,* Perennial Books, 1977.

RJC April 1979

OUR MUSLIM NEIGHBOURS

William Burridge

OUR MUSLIM NEIGHBOURS

No one who has ever lived in Muslim lands can ever forget that moment each day in the first glimmer of dawn when the clear cry of the muezzin from the tower of the mosque echoes across the hilltop village or over the white, shallow-domed roofs of a densely packed town.

'God is most great!' sings out the muezzin, 'God is most great! I testify there is no God but he...' And the world wakes to a new day in a call to an ardent act of faith and orientation towards God.

This awareness of God is at the heart of the life and religion of Islam. There are about one million Muslims in Britain today, though for them there is no cry of the muezzin calling them to prayer.

Submission to God

Life itself begins for a Muslim in an aura of awareness of God. Into the ears of the new-born babe are whispered those words of the muezzin: 'God is great! There is no God but he!...Come, to prayer, to prosperity...' From its first moments in this world the baby is ushered on its way to God and into the Muslim way of life.

Everyday life is filled with this awareness; *Bismillah* ('in the name of God') the devout Muslim says before doing anything, and *Insha'allah* ('God willing') when planning ahead.

All this is rooted in belief in the one and only God, who is eternal, all powerful, creator and sustainer of the universe. He knows, sees, and hears everything. He is everywhere. He is kind and merciful. He has provided us with everything. He is the sovereign law-giver, the source of all guidance. He has sent Prophets to guide us and tell us how to obey him and live according to his will, and so find happiness and security.

The Muslim believes in life after death and the Day of Judgement when each will be called on to give account of his conduct here on earth, with the outcome Paradise or Hell. Life on earth is brief, the hereafter eternal.

Men and women are seen as created by God to be his representative on earth ('my existence is witness to God'), designed in harmony with the forces of the universe, endowed with free will and moral responsibility. Man's natural instincts are not evil (Muslims do not believe in original sin) but they must be controlled to comply with the pattern and the rules God has given. The very meaning of the word 'Islam' is 'submission' (to God) and 'Muslim' (from the same root, *s-l-m* in Arabic) means 'one who submits'. In this willing submission faith and conduct are inseparable.

The Five Pillars of Islam

This living faith of Islam is specially fostered by the 'Five Pillars', practices obligatory on all Muslims.

The first is the Declaration of Faith (*Shahādah*): 'I declare that there is no god but God. He is one and has no partner. I declare that Muhammad is his servant and his messenger.' Making this simple profession of faith is itself sufficient to make one a Muslim.

The second is set prayer five times a day (*Salāt*), at dawn, midday, late afternoon, sunset and late evening. This bears out the primary importance of prayer in the life of the Muslim. He pauses at these times to renew his sense of the presence of God, in humble submission to him, asking for mercy, light and forgiveness, facing the while towards Mecca (or *Makka*), the great shrine of Islamic faith, and kneeling and bowing to give his prayer a more total expression. Setting aside time for formal prayer five times a day demands ideally an interruption of work or other occupations. It is, indeed, edifying when one happens, say, to be reading in Islamic Council of Europe offices to see a member of staff leave his desk and kneel down, absorbed for a few moments in the joy of the midday prayer. The rules for the observance of *salāt* allow a certain flexibility, so that if a person is legitimately prevented from saying the prayers within the prescribed periods they are to be said at some other time, even grouping several of the five prayers together. This flexibility is especially useful to our Muslim neighbours, who have not the advantage of living where the pattern of public and private life is geared to the observances of Islam as it is in Muslim countries.

Awareness of God the Creator to whom all things belong suggests the third 'pillar', the duty of giving a percentage of one's wealth annually for the benefit of the poor. This is seen not only as a duty for the giver but also the right of the poor, an act of gratitude to God and a means of worshipping him.

The fourth 'pillar' is the month of fasting, *Ramadan*. During *Ramadan* Muslims fast from dawn to sunset from all food and drink (and from smoking) for thirty consecutive days: an act of worship, self-discipline and purification.

The fifth 'pillar' is the pilgrimage to Mecca, obligatory on all who are able to do it at least once in a lifetime. It takes place from 8 to 13 of *Dhil Hijja*, the last month of the Muslim calendar. Hundreds of thousands of pilgrims, all dressed in a plain white robe (with an added long white veil for women) spend these days in prayerful massed visits to the holy places that are the original home of Islam in and around Mecca. For here, Muslims believe, Abraham lived and here Muhammad was born and became God's messenger.

During the pilgrimage, camels, sheep and other animals are sacrificed at Mina, in the vicinity of Mecca, to recall the story of Abraham and his son and as a symbol of the pilgrims' readiness to give all they have and are for God and the faith of Islam. At the same time Muslims round the world keep the festival of the sacrifices (*'id al − adha*), sharing in the pilgrims' remembrance of Abraham's act of submission to the will of God.

The pilgrimage is not simply an optional devotional extra. It is a supreme act of religion, setting a seal on the person's life and marking him for the rest of his days with the revered title of pilgrim, making him, after his return home, a link, as it were, with the sacred home of Islam. One pilgrim has described it as 'an occasion of great happiness and blessings, to pray in the sacred house of the *Ka'ba*, to see the holy places and meet Muslims of many races − a great family reunion.'

There are other feasts in the Muslim calendar as well as *'id al-adha*, such as the festival of the breaking of the fast (*'id-al-fitr*) at the close of Ramadan. This is a day of high festivity. The head of each family makes a donation (*sadaquah-al-fitr*) on behalf of each one of its members so that the poor can all buy food and join fully in the festival. In Britain a few years ago the donation was fixed at 60p per head in every family and in this way the local community produced a large sum for distribution to the poor.

Prayers of thanksgiving for all blessings of the Islamic faith and way of life are said at home and in the mosque.

The mosque plays an important role as the community hub of prayer and instruction. Friday, although not necessarily a day of 'rest' like Sunday or the Sabbath, is the special day for attending the mosque at midday.

An *imam*, a community leader (there are no priests nor clergy properly so-called in Islam) normally stands in front of the congregation facing, like them, the semi-circular recess (the *mihrab*) which marks the direction of Mecca and leads them in the prayers and gestures which accompany them, a sequence of bowing, kneeling and so on. There is a pulpit (*minbar*) with its high flight of steps and opposite a lectern on which the book of the Qur'an rests.

Here, by way of a sample, is the opening prayer:

Praise belongs to God, Lord of the Worlds, the Compassionate, the Merciful, King of the Day of Judgement. It is you we worship and whom we ask for help. Guide us on the straight path, the path of those whom you have favoured, not the path of those who incur your anger nor of those who go astray.

Besides the prayers there is a sermon.

Muhammad

So far we have barely mentioned Muhammad, a thing which to a Muslim would be unpardonable. We have deliberately waited until now because there is always the danger of non-Muslims thinking of Muhammad as the 'founder' of Islam and even of committing the mistake, appalling to Muslims, of describing Islam as 'Muhammadanism'.

Islam is not conceived by Muslims as a new religion founded in the days of Muhammad but of one in the continuity with God's revelation in the Old Testament. They believe that Muhammad is the last and final one of the line of Prophets chosen by God for that purpose: Abraham, Isaac, Jacob, Moses, David, John, Jesus, Muhammad.

He is, of course, the supreme personality in the history of Islam and his name is never mentioned by devout Muslims without the reverent addition, 'Blessings of God (or *'Allah'*, the word for God in Arabic) and peace be upon him.'

Muhammad was born around the year 570. He belonged to the Banu Hashim, part of the Quraysh tribe, one of the many pagan tribes that lived in Mecca. The clan was highly respected and had influential connections but was not one of the ruling families, and the young Muhammad probably knew the privations of poverty.

His father died before Muhammad was born; his mother died when he was four years old. He was cared for first by his grandfather and then by uncles. He had a beduin nurse with whom he led a nomad life. He was later employed by a widow whose camels plied the trade routes from Mecca to Damascus. He married the widow, Khadija; he was twenty-five years old, she was forty. After her death he married again. He had a reputation for honesty in business and he earned the nicknames 'Trusty' and 'Truthful'. He liked going off quietly on his own to a cave in the neighbourhood of Mecca and it is there, with a religious experience he had one day at prayer, that any study in depth of Muhammad and Islam has really to begin. Whatever the exact nature of that experience, it was certainly the starting point of the particular spiritual perspectives and values with which Muhammad brought Islam and the Muslim community into being.

The Mecca of his earlier years had built up in Muhammad spiritual, if ill-defined, aspirations. He was bewildered by the hotchpotch of pagan gods and occult practices. Fragments of Christian and Jewish beliefs had been brought to Mecca by merchants and travellers. They may have nurtured in Muhammad a desire for the kind of God of whom they spoke. At the same time He was increasingly disgusted by the materialism and corruption which had come with a sudden wave of prosperity as the imperial wars of Persia and Byzantium had unexpectedly diverted lucrative trade routes towards Mecca. He was distressed, too, by the neglect of the poor in the midst of this growing wealth. It all led him to turn in on himself and spend more time in the quiet of his beloved cave.

It was in 610, when he was forty, that he had the religious experience that changed his life and was eventually to change human history. Muhammad believed that he had been given a message from God. He was at first bewildered and terrified. He fled home from the cave. He wondered whether he was not the victim of illusion or even diabolical deception. Under the strain he even experienced a period of physical collapse. Khadijah was convinced his vision was genuine and did much to reassure him. Muhammad regained his composure and claimed to hear words declaring that he had been chosen by God to proclaim his message.

There ensued a period of spiritual aridity and a sense of abandonment by God. Later came further communication:

By the light of day and by the night as it spreads out your Lord has not abandoned you nor has he thrust you aside. Yes, in the end your Lord will be bounteous to you and you shall be satisfied. Did he not find you an orphan and give you a home? Did he not find you in error and guide you to

truth? He found you in need and made you independent…
As for the favours of the Lord, proclaim them far and wide.

Thereupon Muhammad embarked on his mission, beginning with his family and friends. The main outline of his message was: There is one God, creator of heaven and earth. He alone is to be worshipped. It is his will that men take care of the poor and be honest in their dealings. The just will be rewarded, the wicked punished. God's judgement will come even now as well as on the last day.

Muhammad met all kinds of opposition, even physical assault, from the Meccans, who clung to their idolatrous and pagan ways. Eventually, in 622 AD, he moved to Medina with his followers, an event which marks Year One of the Muslim era.

At Medina Islam grew. Armed conflicts took place with the Meccans. In 630 AD (AH 8) Muhammad and his followers returned to Mecca, triumphant and forgiving. The great cube-shaped building, the *Ka'ba*, in Mecca, already a place of religious pilgrimage, now became the heart and shrine of Islam.

Soon, the world of Islam was extended by conquest in holy war throughout the Middle East, along North Africa and even into Europe. The devout Muslim will insist that Islam did not build empires for its own sake. But Islam believes it is possible to realise God's sovereignty on earth by and through the Islamic state. The idea that 'religion and politics must be kept separate' would make no sense in a Muslim country.

Everything Muhammad said and did shows an unwavering intent to carry out the will of God. The growth of his conviction that his message came from God formed a pattern of personal spiritual pilgrimage. God, the Almighty and Unique, became totally central to his thinking and activity. He lived in a sense of wonder at his encounter with God. There is a joy and exuberance and an agony of desire to express the inexpressible about God. One detects in the spirituality of Islam successive stages of prayer, the role of silence and recollection, the transformation brought about by the first sensing of the presence of God and the urge, which contemplation engenders, to make known the works of God.

The Message

For Muslims Muhammad is both the model of what a Muslim should be and the messenger God used to give them – and indeed, they believe, the whole world – religious beliefs as well as laws and regulations covering every aspect of private and public life.

These are found first and foremost in the *Qur'an* (Koran).

For Muslims the *Qur'an* is in the strictest sense the word of God. They believe that it was dictated word for word to Muhammad by the Angel Gabriel. He was told to recite the text, while his companions committed what they heard to memory, and kept it alive by often repeating it. Others learnt it from them. The very word *Qur'an* comes from the Arabic for 'to read aloud or recite'. These revelations came to Muhammad from time to time across a period of twenty-three years. Some years after Muhammad's death they were all gathered together from those who remembered them and from bits of parchment, bone and so on on which they had been written down. Thus the *Qur'an*, Islam's sacred book, was compiled.

The revealed text was in Arabic and so it is in Arabic that it is preserved, as a sacred and inviolable message communicated by God. The *Qur'an* consists of 114 chapters *(suras)* with a total of 6666 verses *('ayat)*; a bit shorter than the New Testament. Although readily available as a printed book the ideal is to be able to recite it, or at least parts of it, by heart. Someone who can do the whole *Qur'an* by heart is called a *hafiz*. There are many famous and immensely popular reciters, called *Qari*, masters of the special sing-song tones. Listening to them is a joy for Muslims. Nowadays they can do so on cassettes and records, too.

The *Qur'an* has its place in every good Muslim home. The father of a devout Muslim family will take the *Qur'an*, wrapped reverently in velvet, from its special shelf before breakfast and read from it to his wife and children sitting round him, careful not to turn their backs towards the Holy Book, barefoot out of respect for it. 'By the morning hours,' says the *Qur'an*, 'and by the night when it is stillest, thy Lord has not forsaken thee.'

Often a child's first reading lesson at home is from the *Qur'an* and many Muslim parents are eager to arrange for evening and weekend classes where their children can learn to recite it.

The *Qur'an* however is not the complete account of the Muslim rule of life. In matters not covered by it divine guidance is sought in the sayings and actions of Muhammad, for they too are seen as a revelation of God's wishes for mankind. These are known as the *hadith*. Early in the history of Islam enormous pains were taken to collect these sayings and actions and sort out the ones that were authentic, which had been witnessed by Muhammad's companions and faithfully handed down. All this may be supplemented by unanimously agreed clarifications made by the leading scholars of the worldwide Muslim community. Although the community (the *umma*) has no 'ecclesiastical' structure, every Muslim has a deep sense of belonging to it by faith and practice. One of the *hadith* says that the community will 'never agree on an error'.

We have already mentioned the provisions regarding times of prayer and the observances laid down by the Five Pillars. We may add other duties such as hospitality (especially keeping an open door for members of the family group), protection of the weak and of orphans. There are certain prohibitions derived from the *Qur'an* and Islamic tradition. Pork, alcohol, gambling and lending or taking money at interest are all forbidden.

The Muslim family

The best place to see how Islam is lived out from day to day is the Muslim family. The family for Muslims is truly the nucleus of society, all the more so because 'family' does not mean only parents and children, but a closely knit group of relatives, the 'extended' family.

Islamic tradition insists on high moral and educational standards. Parents, says the *Qur'an,* must meet their family obligations scrupulously but with kindness and justice. Children must love and respect their parents, especially their mother. Although the *Qur'an* designates the father as mainly in charge in the home, it is the mother who is most responsible for shaping the minds of the children, bringing them up with an attachment to the spiritual and social values of Islam. To us, Muslim parents may seem to be rather strict. But they are not ruling by the rod but bringing up the children with deep love and reverence for all that Islam stands for and forming a bond which unites the whole Muslim community.

The family and extended family faithful to Islam impart an outlook which is often the very opposite of that of the permissive British society around them. Islam stands for chastity outside marriage and faithfulness in marriage. It believes in discipline and obedience as well as love in the upbringing of children. It insists on modesty in dress. In principle, it is against co-education and sex education classes in schools.

The rights of women

It is sometimes said that in Islam women have no rights. In fact, Muslims proudly point to the provisions laid down in the *Qur'an* 1400 years ago which spell out the spiritual, intellectual, social and economic rights of women. Islam says, for instance, 'It is the duty of every Muslim, male and female, to seek knowledge.' There are careful regulations in regard to women concerning social rights, ownership, business transactions, free use of income, participation in politics and questions of rightful inheritance.

At the same time Islam does give great emphasis to the indispensable role of the woman in the home and insists on the man's place as head of the family and his special role in the affairs of the extended family. Government and public affairs in Muslim countries are dominated by men.

Islam sees acts of religion and the happenings of everyday life as one great act of worship of God by mankind in this world. There is in the Islamic faith a wealth of sound understanding about man's relationship with and duty to God as an individual and as a member of society.

Christians and Muslims

Christians and Muslims have many things in common. First, of course, faith in the same God, the one God, who created the world and brings his creatures to their perfection. From this follows the respect both share for the dignity and rights of every individual human being.

Let's take a closer look at Islam's outlook on Christianity. Muslims regard the Scriptures, Old and New Testament, as originally a message from God, but hold that the text has become distorted. We have referred to the *Qur'an's* reverence for the prophets and the special place it gives to Christ. But Muslims regard Jesus as just a great prophet and reject his divinity. His crucifixion is also denied ('They slew him not, and they crucified him not' it is said in the *Qur'an*), and therefore his resurrection. They also reject the Holy Trinity.

But the reasons given in the *Qur'an* and the *hadith* for denying the doctrines of the Incarnation and the Trinity have led Christian scholars to believe that they had not been properly understood by Muhammad. They point out that the Christians he came across were ill-instructed and influenced by current heresies condemned by the Church.

One must note with joy the reverence Muslims have for our Lady. The texts concerning her declare her ever a virgin, and speak of her miraculous motherhood of Christ (usually referred to as 'Jesus son of Mary' in the *Qur'an*) and her total sinlessness. In the *Qur'an* and the commentaries on it there are many passages about our Lady, some corresponding to the Gospel and some to early Christian apocryphal stories.

To sum up:

Islam shares with Christianity belief in:
1. One God;
2. The last judgement and future life;
3. The resurrection of the dead;
4. The value of prayer, fasting and almsdeeds;

5. The virginity of our Lady;

6. Angels;

7. The existence of evil – the devil;

8. It gives a special place to our Lord, but only as a prophet.

Islam differs from Christianity:

1. It does not accept the doctrine of the Trinity.

2. It rejects the divinity of Christ.

3. It rejects his death on the Cross.

4. It rejects the claims of the Catholic Church.

Both religions are expansionist: the Catholic Church through mission, Islam through *Da'wah*, or calling.

Both, up to the present, have confronted each other; now, there is a growing understanding of the need for an ecumenical approach.

Islam is still, on the whole, fundamentalist; it takes the *Qur'an* as literally God's word without modification. There is, however, a growing feeling of the necessity for *aggiornamento*, for taking the core of the message of Islam and expressing it in different frameworks, without altering what is essential to it.

Divisions in Islam

To complete this account of Islam one would have to talk about the various sects that have arisen in the Muslim world. The main body, 90% of all Muslims, is made up of *Sunnites.* They derive their title from *sunna,* the Arabic word for custom or usage. The Sunnites claim to remain faithful to the practice and doctrine of Muhammad and the early Muslim community. As crises and divisions arose in the history of Islam, the majority steered a middle course between extremes and labelled themselves 'the people of the *sunna* and the community.' The main minority group, the *Shi'ites*, who make up the overwhelming majority in Iran, is itself split into a large number of very different Muslim sects – the *Zaidis* and the *Ismailis* for example – including some sometimes considered beyond the borders of Islam, such as the *Druse*. Many Sunnites are quite unaware of the existence of sects; those who are are often keenly sensitive about this diversity in Islam.

There are some 12,000 members of the Ahmadiyya Movement in Britain, who regard themselves as representing true Islam but who are repudiated by both Sunnites and Shi'ites.

There are cultural differences between Muslims, contrary to the idea some have in the West that they all come from Arabia. For instance the Muslims in Britain are mostly from Pakistan, India, Bangladesh, and East Africa; there are also some from Cyprus, Turkey, the Middle East, Malaysia and Indonesia. Although all firmly rooted in Islam and its observances and ideals, they come from a variety of backgrounds, react differently to the novelty of their surroundings and bring with them the particular customs of their home countries.

All that we have said is not meant simply to satisfy our curiosity about Muslim neighbours and fellow citizens. What should interest us most is the fact that Islam, and therefore the lives of our Muslim neighbours, contains so much that is true and holy. This was recognized by the Catholic Church at the second Vatican Council (1962-5), at which she committed herself to seek collaboration and dialogue with Muslims. In August 1985 Pope John Paul II declared that

> Dialogue between Christians and Muslims is today more necessary than ever...In a world which desires unity and peace, but which experiences instead a thousand tensions

and conflicts, should not believers seek friendship between all men and women and all peoples and nations, who, after all, make up one single community on earth'? All have one and the same origin and one and the same final end: the God who made them and who waits for them, and who will finally gather them all together into one.

(Casablanca, 18.8.85)

The best witness Christians can give to Muslims of their faith is to be seen to be people in whose lives prayer, awareness of God and fidelity to him and his commandments take priority.

Some useful names and addresses

The following organizations provide useful resources and information for Catholic teachers, clergy and lay people involved in inter-faith dialogue:

The **R.C. Committee for Other Faiths** was established in 1984. Its purpose is to help Catholics deepen their own faith by promoting a greater awareness and understanding of other faiths through dialogue, prayer and action in light of the Church's teaching. Chairman: Bishop Charles Henderson. Secretary: Miss Celia Blackden, Park House, 6A Cresswell Park, Blackheath, London SE3 9RD, telephone 01-318 1094.

The **Westminster Interfaith Programme** tries to bring the aims expressed by the R.C. Committee for Other Faiths into reality by means of meetings and talks, visits to places of worship, interfaith prayer vigils, concerts and pilgrimages. The coordinator is Brother Daniel Faivre SG, 2 Church Avenue, Southall, Middlesex UB2 4DH, telephone 01-843 0690.

The **Birmingham Multi-Faith Resource Unit** (MUFRU) was founded as a result of three years' research initiated by the Roman Catholic Bishops' Conference 1978 to consider some initiative to establish relationships between Christians and non-Christians in Britain. The Conference includes lectures, seminars, group work visits to synagogues, mosques, temples and centres, all combining to provide opportunities for people of different religions and cultures to deepen their understanding of each other. For further details contact Dr Mary Hall, 1 College Walk, Selly Oak, Birmingham B29 6LE, telephone 021-472 0139.

Much useful help and information is available from Muslim sources. The primary object of some of these organizations is to help the Muslim community to preserve its religious heritage by providing educational materials for use with Muslim children, but they also work for better relations between Christians and Muslims and provide books and pamphlets presenting Islam to a non-Muslim readership.

Islam Book Centre, 120 Drummond Street, London NW1 2HL, telephone 01-388 0710. A small but well stocked bookshop with materials ranging from editions of the Qur'an and academic works to books and games for children (including 'Snakes and Ladders' adapted for Muslim children!). A free catalogue and order form is available.

Islamic Council of Europe, 16 Grosvenor Crescent, London SW1, telephone 01-235 9832.

Islamic Cultural Centre and **London Central Mosque,** 146 Park Road, London NW8, telephone 01-724 3363. Publishes literature, posters, lesson materials for all age ranges, some leaflets and books free.

Islamic Foundation, 223 London Road, Leicester LE2 1ZE, telephone 0533-700725. Produces over one hundred books and pamphlets on Islam, as well as audio-visual resources, games for children, maps and posters. A free catalogue and order form is available from the Islamic Foundation Publications Unit, Unit 9, The Old Dunlop Factory, 62 Evington Valley Road, Leicester, telephone 0533-734860.

Islamic Youth Council, 52 Fieldgate Street, London El. There are branches of the Islamic Youth Movement in Birmingham, Bradford, Nottingham, Rochdale, Manchester and Walsall.

Muslim Educational Trust, 130 Strand Green Road, London N4 3RZ, telephone 01-272 8502. Publishes books, posters and cards, including a free leaflet *Islam – a brief guide.*

Muslim Women's Association, 146 Park Road, London NW8.

UK Islamic Mission, 202 North Gower Street, London NW1 2LY, telephone 01-387 2157. An organization devoted to the maintenance of sound knowledge and the faithful practice of Islam in the Muslim community, and to the promotion of friendly relations between Muslims and non-Muslims.

Books and pamphlets

The literature on Islam is extensive. Readers for whom this booklet has provided an introduction will find the following titles of interest.

A. J. Arberry (translator), *The Koran,* Oxford University Press, 1984, a reprint of the earlier *The Koran Interpreted.*

Alfred Guillaume, *Islam,* Penguin Books, first published 1954.

CAN WE TRUST THE GOSPELS?

John Wijngaards

Michael Nazir-Ali, *Islam, A Christian Perspective*, Paternoster Press, 1983.

Kenneth Cragg, *Muhammad and the Christian: A Question of Response*, Darton, Longman and Todd, 1984.

Kenneth Cragg, *The Call of the Minaret*, second revised edition, Collins, 1986.

The Catholic Truth Society pamphlet by Edward Hulmes, *Muhammad* (B 598) is a short introduction to the life and work of the prophet of Islam specially written for Christians.

There are also two useful CTS pamphlets on the relationship between the great world religions and Christianity: *Is one religion as good as another?* (R177) by Gavin d'Costa and *Other Faiths: What does the Church teach?* (R179), a selection from the documents of Vatican II, recent encyclicals and Papal homilies prepared by the R.C. Committee for Other Faiths.

When Christians quote from the Gospels, Muslims often reply:

> The text you are quoting from is not the true Gospel. The original Gospel of Jesus Christ has been lost. Past generations of Christians have corrupted your Scriptures so that now they are useless.

Muslims are so convinced about this that meaningful communication with them usually breaks down at this point. How to explain what we believe regarding Jesus Christ, when Muslims are convinced that the original Gospels presented another Jesus? Whether spoken or unspoken, the suspicion, if not the accusation, is always there: 'You are relying on Scriptures that have been falsified!'

Such allegations also appear in print. Recently a book was published with the title *Jesus Prophet of Islam*. In line with common Muslim thinking, the author contends that Jesus presented himself as no more than an ordinary prophet, that he never died on the Cross (he was miraculously spirited away by angels), that he announced the coming of Muhammad. Present-day Christian doctrine is a heresy, deliberately introduced in later years. And these heretics, he says, pointing an accusing finger, were prepared to mutilate the Scriptures too. They even introduced false writings in order to support their opinions:

The books into which Jesus's teaching had gone were either completely destroyed, suppressed or changed in order to avoid any blatant contradiction with their own, new doctrine…The original teaching in its totality has disappeared and is irrevocably lost.

Not content with pronouncing such a general indictment, the author pinpoints a precise historical beginning to the process of falsification:

In 325 AD, the famous Council of Nicea was held. The doctrine of the Trinity was declared to be the official doctrine of the Pauline Church, and one of the consequences of this decision was that out of the three hundred or so gospels extant at the time, four were chosen as the official gospels of the Church. The remaining gospels, including the gospel of Barnabas, were ordered to be destroyed. An edict was issued stating that anyone found in possession of an unauthorised gospel would be put to death. This was the first well-organised attempt to remove all the records of Jesus's original teaching, whether in human beings or in books[1].

For those familiar with historical fact, such gratuitous assertions will easily be shrugged off. What to reply to a person who believes that London lies in Libya? But it may not be so easy for Christians who have not studied theology or Church history. They may not know what answer to give when talking to their Muslim friends or what to make of such Muslim publications. For their sake I shall put together some facts and arguments to show that our Gospels have not been falsified. But first it may be useful to ask: where did Muslims get the idea that our Gospels have been tampered with?

The origin of a myth

In the Qur'an Muslims are told to respect the Gospel revealed to Jesus Christ and read by Christians. The Qur'an presupposes that the Gospel possessed by Christians is in fact identical with the original one proclaimed by Jesus[2]. In the first four centuries after Muhammad (600 – 1000 AD) no Muslim theologian seriously contended that the Gospel texts were not authentic. They might accuse Christians of giving a wrong interpretation to the words; they would not dispute the words themselves. As studies of Muslim apologetics have shown, it was only with Ibn-Khazem, who died at Cordoba in 1064, that the charge of falsification was born[3].

Ibn-Khazem ruled the south of Spain for some time as the vizier of the caliph, waging many civil wars on his behalf. He also took part in theological discussions. Belonging to the so-called Zahiric school, he strongly opposed the Shi'ites. 'Both in religion and in politics he was a hard and intransigent fighter. Whoever dared to resist him hurt himself as by running against a rock. His pen was as devastating a weapon as the sword of the warrior. Because of his fanaticism he failed to attract disciples or found a school. But his writings were very influential in later times'[4].

In his defence of Islam against Christians, Ibn-Khazem came up against the contradictions between the Qur'an and the Gospels. One obvious example was the Qur'anic text, 'They slew him not, and they crucified him not' (Sura 4,156). 'Since the Qur'an must be true,' Ibn-Khazem argued, 'it must be the conflicting Gospel texts that are false. But Muhammad tells us to respect the Gospel. Therefore, the present text must have been falsified by the Christians.' His argument was not based on historical facts, but purely on his own reasoning and on his wish to safeguard the truth of the Qur'an[5]. Once he was on this path, nothing could stop him from pursuing this accusation. In fact, it seemed the easiest way to attack the opponents. 'If we prove the falsehood of their books, they lose the arguments they take from them'[6]. This led him eventually to make the cynical statement: 'The Christians lost the revealed Gospel except for a few traces which God has left intact as argument against them'[7].

Later writers took up the same reasoning, enlarged it and embellished it. The falsification of the Bible was thus asserted by Salikh Ibn-al-Khusain (died 1200), Ahmad al-Qarafi (died 1285), Sa'id Ibn-Khasan (died 1320), Muhammad Ibn-Abi-Talib (died 1327), Ibn-Taimija (died 1328) and many others. From then on it became a fixed ingredient of Muslim apologetics.

These same authors designate the Emperor Constantine and Paul as the chief falsifiers. Constantine, whose personality is blurred for them with the Council of Nicea, is said to have invented the story of Jesus's crucifixion for political reasons and to have reduced the number of gospels to four. About Paul many fantastic stories are recounted. According to one version, Paul was a great enemy of Christianity who wanted to destroy it utterly. First he tried violence, but when this did not succeed, he decided to go about it in a different way. He pretended conversion and allowed himself to be baptised. His intention was to ruin Christianity from within. To make sure that he would make a lasting impression on the Christians, he wished to be considered a martyr. So he invented the story that Christ had appeared to him during the night and had requested him to sacrifice himself at the foot of a mountain. On the day before his death he called the three main Christian kings and gave to each a secret revelation: to the first that Christ is God's son; to the second that Mary was God's wife; to the third that God is three. When the sun rose next morning Paul came out of his cell in a grey mantle carrying a knife. He sacrificed himself with his own hands. The people watched him and believed him to be a saint. This is how Christians received their false doctrines and how they became divided into different sects[8]. According to other stories Paul was a Jewish king, or a monk living in Rome 150 years after Christ. All versions agree in calling him a crafty falsifier, who feigned conversion to corrupt the Christian community from the inside.

These fables about Constantine and Paul seem to have arisen from a mixture of anti-Christian Jewish sources, Persian legends and Marcionite writings[9]. It is not difficult to show that they make no historical sense. Paul lived from c. 5 – 67 AD, preached the same doctrine as the other Apostles and wrote many of the New Testament Letters. Constantine was the Roman Emperor from 312 – 337 AD. He gave Christians the freedom to practise their religion, but he did not invent the crucifixion or tamper with the Gospels. The Council of Nicea which gathered from May 20 to August 25 in 324 AD did not decree anything regarding apocryphal writings. The 300 bishops who participated argued about the understanding of the Scriptures, not about what was Scripture or was not. They were in full agreement regarding the text. All these are historical facts.

Knowing the cause of a sickness is the first step to its cure. Muslims often read only their own literature and since these will keep repeating the old accusations, they may be firmly convinced they are right. A frog in a well may believe he has seen the ocean. There is no solution. Genuine progress in dialogue is only possible when a person, whether Christian or Muslim, is prepared to step outside the vicious circle of self-enforced prejudice by facing objective facts.

This leads us on to consider the Gospels themselves. Can we find out what the original text was, the precise words of the inspired writings as they were written down in the period between 50 and 90 AD? Many scientists have devoted their whole lives to this question. The science of 'text criticism' has studied many ancient writings, among them the books of the New Testament. I shall endeavour to explain in a few paragraphs what is, in actual fact, a complicated and painstaking procedure.

In Christ's time all books and letters had to be written out by hand. When the New Testament writings had been completed, they could only be spread to the various Christian communities by taking hand-written copies of them. Such a copy is called a 'manuscript' (a Latin word that means 'written by hand'). The material used in those days was papyrus, an inferior quality of paper made of reed. Because the sacred writings would be handled frequently – for private reading as well as for the Sunday celebrations – the original text and the earliest copies would soon be tattered and worn. They were being replaced continuously by new copies.

In the fourth century AD a better material was found, namely parchment. This parchment was manufactured from strips of sheepskin that were scraped and tanned and sewn together to form scrolls. Obviously, this parchment made of leather was much more expensive, but its advantage consisted in its being almost indestructible. Gradually more and more New Testament copies were made on parchment scrolls, or on 'codices', i.e. books in which the sheets of parchment were piled up one on top of the other (as our books are arranged today). There were also improvements in the writing. During the first century every Greek letter was written as a capital (the so-called majuscule script). Later a more differentiated style arose (the minuscule script). When scientists find an ancient manuscript, they first determine its age, then transcribe it as faithfully as possible and study all its characteristics. The text preserved in a particular manuscript is then compared to that found in other ones.

To study the New Testament writings, scientists have a wealth of material at their disposal. Of the Greek text (remember that the New Testament was written in Greek) there are no less than 4680 manuscripts. 68 of them are papyri, 241 majuscule parchments, 2533 minuscule parchments and 1838 lectionaries (collections of Scripture texts for reading on Sundays). Then there are more than 6000 manuscripts of ancient translations in such languages as Latin, Syriac, Coptic, Gothic, Armenian, Ethiopic, Georgian, Nubian, Arabic, Persian and Slavonic. A third source for comparison are quotations of scriptural texts found with more than 220 Church Fathers and theologians.

Some of these texts are very old. One of the papyri, known as P52, contains fragments of St John's Gospel. It has been dated as 130 AD, which means that this copy of the Gospel was written hardly forty years after the original. Another famous example is the Codex Sinaiticus, which was written in about 350 AD in Egypt. 347 of its leaves have been preserved which cover practically the whole New Testament From comparing the handwriting we can see that three scribes had worked at it.

The nature of the evidence

To compare these thousands of manuscripts and other sources which range roughly from the second to the fourteenth century is a gargantuan task. But it has been done. The repeated copying of the text through the centuries, by different scribes in widely separated places, resulted in small variations creeping into the text. They are known as 'variant readings'. Once such a variant reading had been incorporated, further copies would obviously contain the same variation. By analysing these small differences, scientists have been able to group many manuscripts together, showing that they derive from common ancestor manuscripts. In this way very early versions of the text can be reconstructed with great precision. We know what the text was like at the end of the third century in four streams of transmission: the Alexandrian, Western, Caesarian and Antiochian families. By projecting this further back into the past, the original text that must have antedated these recensions can be arrived at.

The outcome of all these studies has been to establish beyond doubt the authenticity of the New Testament text. We can be absolutely sure that the text we possess is essentially identical to the original writings[10]. Or, to put it in quantitative terms: the small variations that have crept into the text over all these centuries affect only one and a half per cent of the text (one of every sixty words); they rarely make any doctrinal difference. Ninety-eight and a half per cent of the text is certain beyond reasonable doubt.

This proves that the text has not been falsified. Indeed, if anybody at any time had attempted such a falsification, this could immediately be detected. Imagine that a wealthy banker in Singapore wrote a last will describing how his property should be divided after fifty years. Imagine that he had five children, each of whom made a copy of this will and had it with him while migrating to different parts of the world: London, Cape Town, Los Angeles, Sydney and Rio de Janeiro. Each of these children again had five children who all made copies of the document possessed by their parents. Again, they too had five children each, who in turn made copies of the document. Now even supposing that the original will of their great-grandfather in Singapore was lost, by a comparison of the many copies that had been made in so many different places the original text could with certainty be established. If any of the children or grandchildren had tried to change the text, his deception would immediately be exposed by its deviation from what the other copies showed. In the same way, any attempt at falsifying the Gospel text would immediately show up in its discrepancy from the many thousands of manuscripts that retain independent copies.

The Buddhist king Ashoka who ruled in India from 273 to 240 BC promulgated a unique, humanitarian constitution. He ordered it to be inscribed in many places throughout his empire: on rocks, on pillars, on the walls of caves. Because more than thirty-five of such inscriptions have been preserved, we know with certainty what Ashoka's original constitution was. Even if one of the stone carvers had wanted to falsify Ashoka's text and so deceive us, we could prove the deception by comparison with the other versions. The Gospels were the constitution of the Early Church, copied in thousandfold from the earliest days. If a falsification had taken place, it could not fail to show up.

H. K. Moulton, who spent more than forty years studying the manuscripts, may be quoted by way of summary at this point. After stating that the smaller variations between texts do in no single case mean a loss of Christian doctrine, he says:

> When all the documents have been sifted and rigidly examined, we find that essentially they agree…The textual critic leads us back from our present printed Scripture through long and sometimes round-about paths to the New Testament writers themselves. He gives us substantially

what they wrote, rigorously tested and objectively approved…
No book has ever had its text so vigorously examined as the
New Testament has. No fabrication could have survived
such thorough testing without falling apart…We can trust
our Source-Book; it has been weighed in the balance and
not found wanting[11].

Guardians of Tradition

Thus it has been shown that the Christians from the earliest
times onwards have faithfully preserved the revealed doctrines
they had received. This should not surprise us. We know how
anxious they were to guard the treasures which God had
entrusted to them. As early as the year 50 AD St Paul writes:
'Brethren, stand firm and hold to the traditions which you were
taught by us' (2 Thess. 2: 15). 'Maintain the traditions as I have
handed them on to you' (1 Cor. 11: 2). 'I handed on to you
what I also received, that Christ died for our sins, as written in
the Scriptures; that he was buried and that he was raised to life
three days later…This is what we all preach, and this is what
you believe…You are saved by the Gospel if you hold firmly to
it' (1 Cor. 15: 3–4, 11,2).

The early Christians were as anxious as we are to know
what Christ has said and done. The Greeks and Romans had
developed quite high standards of historical writing. They knew
this should report objective facts, proved by eyewitness accounts
and original documents. Modern scholars judge that several of
the ancient historians were trustworthy and accurate in the
writings which they left us. Herodotus, Thucydides, Polybius
and Tacitus were outstanding; Josephus, Caesar, Polybius and
Livy noteworthy. Even if some people were careless about it, the

early Christian writers certainly knew what accurate recording involved[12]. Consequently, we should take Luke's claim seriously when he says he has consulted eyewitnesses (Lk. 1: 2) and then continues: 'Because I have carefully studied all these matters from their beginning, I thought it would be good to write an orderly account of them for you. I do this so that you will know the full truth about everything which you have been taught' (Lk. 1: 3–4). Christians have always wanted to know the full truth about everything which they have been taught.

A new beginning

Christians and Muslims share many beliefs in common. Both accept only one God, the Creator and Source of all Revelation, the Merciful Judge who will punish the wicked and reward the good. With materialism gaining the upper hand and in many parts of the world, it is important that believers stress what they have in common rather than intensify mutual opposition. This means that unfounded prejudice on both sides should be removed. In February 1976, 1200 delegates from sixty countries took part in a seminar on 'Islamic-Christian Dialogue'. The Christians asked the Muslims to make a deeper study of the New Testament and to drop the charge of falsification. Dialogue requires that each party accepts the authenticity of the other person's Scriptures on which his faith is based[13].

Many of the great Muslim thinkers have, indeed, accepted the authenticity of the New Testament text. Listing the names of these men seems a fitting conclusion to this essay. Their testimony proves that Christian–Muslim dialogue need not for ever be stymied by the allegation introduced by Ibn-Khazem. Two great historians, Al-Mas'udi (died 956) and Ibn-Khaldun (died 1406), held the authenticity of the Gospel text. Four well-known theologians agreed with this: Ali at-Tabari (died 855), Qasim al-Khasani (died 860), 'Amr al-Ghakhiz (died 869) and, last but not least, the famous Al-Ghazzali (died 1111)[14]. Their view is shared by Abu Ali Husain Ibn Sina, who is known in the West as Avicenna (died 1037). Bukhari (died 870), who acquired a great name by his collection of early traditions, quoted the Qur'an itself (Sura 3,72.78) to prove that the text of the Bible was not falsified[15]. Finally, Muhammad Abduh Sayyid Ahmad Khan, a religious and social reformer of modern times (died 1905), accepted the findings of modern science. He said:

> As far as the text of the Bible is concerned: it has not been altered…No attempt was made to present a diverging text as the authentic one[16].

May God be praised for the witness of these honest men.

NOTES

1. MUHAMMAD ATA UR-RAHIM, *Jesus Prophet of Islam*, Omar Brothers Publications, Singapore 1978, pp. 12, 15 and 40.

2. G. PARRINDER, *Jesus in the Qur'an*, Faber and Faber, London 1965, ch. 15.

3. P. A. PALMIERI *Die Polemik des Islams*, German tr. Holzer, Salzburg 1902; E. FRITSCH, *Islam und Christentum im Mittelalter*, Müller & Seiffert, Breslau 1930; see also: H. HIRSCHFELD, 'Muhammadan Criticism of the Bible'. *Jewish Quarterly Review* 13 (1901) 222–240.

4. F. M. PAREJA, *Islamologia*, Orbis Catholicus, Roma 1951, pp. 460–461.

5. I. DI MATTEO,'Il "takhrif"od alterazione della Bibbia secondo i musulmani', *Bessarione* 38 (1922) 64–111; 223–260; 'Le preteze contradizzioni della S. Scrittura secondo Ibn-Hazm', *Bessarione* 39 (1923) 77–127; E. FRITSCH, op cit., p. 66.

6. IBN KHAZEM, *Kitab al-fasl fi'l-milah wa'l ahwa'l nikhal*, II,6; E. FRITSCH, op cit., p. 55.

7. IBN KHAZEM, ibid.; E. FRITSCH, op. cit., p. 64.

8. Synopsized from AL-QARAFI; E. FRITSCH, op. cit., p. 49.

9. Parallel stories are found in Tustari's Persian version of *Qisas al-anbija* (history of the prophets) in a manuscript dated 1330 AD, and in Ghalal-addin Rumi's *Metnewi*

(the story of a Jewish king and his vizier, 1273 AD); E. FRITSCH, op. cit., pp. 50–65.

10. For a more complete description of text criticism and its conclusions, I recommend: F. G. KENYON, *The Text of the Greek Bible*, London 1937, 1949; L. D. TWILLEY, *The Origin and Transmission of the New Testament*, Edinburgh 1957; V. TAYLOR, *The Text of the New Testament*, London and New York 1961; J. H. GREENLEE, *An Introduction to New Testament Textual Criticism*, Grand Rapids 1964; B. M. METZGER, *The Text of the New Testament*, Oxford 1968.

11. H. K. MOULTON, *Papyrus, Parchment and Print; the story of how the New Testament text has reached us*, London 1967, pp. 9–10, 70–71.

12. A. M. MOSLEY, 'Historical Reporting in the Ancient World', *New Testament Studies* 12 (1965) 10–26.

13. Text of the Final Declaration of the Tripoli Seminar, *L'Osservatore Romano* (English Edition), Feb. 26, 1976, pp. 6–7.

14. I. DI MATTEO, loc. cit. (note 5), AT-TABARI and AL-GHAKHIZ claimed the translations were unfaithful at times; they did not doubt the authenticity of the Greek original. With regard at AL-GHAZZALI, see F. M. PAREJA, op. cit., p. 463.

15. G. PARRINDER, *Jesus in the Qur'an*, Faber and Faber, London 1965; Dutch translation, Ten Have, Baarn 1978, p. 124.

16. M. H. ANANIKIAN, 'The Reforms and Religious Ideas of Sir Sayyid Ahmad Khan'. *The Moslem World* 14 (1934) p. 61.

BACKGROUND

Mgr Coonan's text is really a primer on Muslim belief and practice; it clearly notes the main differences between Christian and Muslim teaching (on the divinity of Jesus Christ and the nature of God, for instance) but does not explain why one might prefer one to the other, nor about different branches and styles of Islam.

William Burridge's *Our Muslim Neighbours* adapts some of Coonan's material. He gives a notably sympathetic account of the social reality of Islam, and portrays (for example) the place of women in Islam in a wholly positive light. He briefly discusses differences within Islam.

Neither of these texts criticises Islam, nor makes any apologetic effort on behalf of Christianity.

Our third text is more constructive. John Wijngaards, a well-known Scripture scholar, addresses head-on the common Muslim allegation that the Gospels have been deliberately altered to conceal the true nature of Jesus. He gives a clear and patient argument for the authenticity of the Gospel text.

CTS ONEFIFTIES

1. FR DAMIEN & WHERE ALL ROADS LEAD · *Robert Louis Stevenson & G K Chesterton*

2. THE UNENDING CONFLICT · *Hilaire Belloc*

3. CHRIST UPON THE WATERS · *John Henry Newman*

4. DEATH & RESURRECTION · *Leonard Cheshire VC & Bede Jarrett OP*

5. THE DAY THE BOMB FELL · *Johannes Siemes SJ & Bruce Kent*

6. MIRACLES · *Ronald Knox*

7. A CITY SET ON A HILL · *Robert Hugh Benson*

8. FINDING THE WAY BACK · *Francis Ripley*

9. THE GUNPOWDER PLOT · *Herbert Thurston SJ*

10. NUNS – WHAT ARE THEY FOR? · *Maria Boulding OSB, Bruno Webb OSB & Jean Cardinal Daniélou SJ*

11. ISLAM, BRITAIN & THE GOSPEL · *John Coonan, William Burridge & John Wijngaards*

12. STORIES OF THE GREAT WAR · *Eileen Boland*

13. LIFE WITHIN US · *Caryll Houselander, Delia Smith & Herbert Fincham*

14. INSIDE COMMUNISM · *Douglas Hyde*

15. COURTSHIP: SOME PRACTICAL ADVICE · *Anon, Hubert McEvoy SJ, Tony Kirwin & Malcolm Brennan*

16. RESURRECTION · *Vincent McNabb OP & B C Butler OSB*

17. TWO CONVERSION STORIES · *James Britten & Ronald Knox*

18. MEDIEVAL CHRISTIANITY · *Christopher Dawson*

19. A LIBRARY OF TALES – VOL 1 · *Lady Herbert of Lea*

20. A LIBRARY OF TALES – VOL 2 · *Eveline Cole & E Kielty*

21. WAR AT HOME AND AT THE FRONT · *"A Chaplain" & Mrs Blundell of Crosby*

22. THE CHURCH & THE MODERN AGE · *Christopher Hollis*

23. THE PRAYER OF ST THÉRÈSE OF LISIEUX · *Vernon Johnson*

24. THE PROBLEM OF EVIL · *Martin D'Arcy SJ*

25. WHO IS ST JOSEPH? · *Herbert Cardinal Vaughan*